CW00553170

CONTENTS

Introduction and Materials   02

SECTION 1: *Creative Surfaces with
Scrim*   05

SECTION 2: *Creative Surfaces for
Three-dimensional Work*   16

SECTION 3: *Creative Surfaces with
Screens, Stencils and Masks*   30

Introduction and Materials

How many times have you been tempted to buy the latest fabric or the latest mixed media product only to find that you really haven't got any idea how to use it? Hopefully you will find some of the answers in this book.

It aims to give you some original ideas for using fabrics such as Lutradur and Tyvek along with acrylic mediums, Xpandaprint and heat transfer foil. There are also new ideas for old favourites such as scrim and Craft Vilene.

My previous book 'Fabulous Surfaces' (published by d4daisy in November 2011) hopefully whetted your appetite for using tissue paper in your work. Further ideas are included here for making use of dressmaking pattern tissue paper.

This book shows you the techniques to create the basic background fabrics and encourages you to expand and explore these by adding hand or machine stitch, beads, mixed media products and techniques to make your own unique piece of work.

The book also contains lots of ideas, many with step-by-step instructions, for making some of the work shown. This is a great way to get started with a new technique.

Use your own favourite range of colours and designs, not necessarily the ones shown on these pages. That way you will find the finished work far more appealing and it will encourage you to take the techniques even further.

< *This shrine is made from Xpandaprint printed onto Lutradur through a Thermofax screen. It was then coloured with fluid transparent acrylics.*

Acrylic mediums and gels

There is a wide range of acrylic mediums and gels available and the choice can be overwhelming. The following products are excellent ones to start with:

- Polymer Medium Gloss: to glaze a coloured surface.
- Regular Gel Medium: ideal for use as an adhesive.
- Light or Regular Molding Paste: great for adding texture; takes colour really well.

Acrylic paint can be added to any of these mediums before application.

Gesso is a good basic ingredient and can always be substituted with household emulsion, if necessary. A small amount of fine sand added to either gesso or emulsion will give you a lovely gritty surface.

Acrylic spray varnish is available in a matt, satin or gloss finish. This is an ideal product for finishing and sealing a surface that is unsuitable for a brush-on sealant.

Materials

Tissue paper

The tissue paper used in the samples throughout this book was dressmaking pattern tissue. (Charity shops are a good source for old patterns.) Not only is it a great way to recycle, it is hardwearing, takes colour really well and dries transparent when coated with an acrylic medium. You can even use it for paper casts.

However, any type of tissue paper can be used for these techniques and it is well worth experimenting with as many types as you can, as the results may differ slightly depending on which colouring agent you use.

Colouring agents

Procion dye, Brusho powders, silk paints, walnut ink, and black writing ink: these are referred to as wet media.

Golden Fluid acrylic paints: these are transparent paints which are ideal when painting over any metallic surface, especially foil, as you are still able to see the rich colours of the foil through the painted surface.

Acrylic paints that come in tubes or pots are generally known as heavy body acrylics.

Xpandaprint/Puff Paint

This is a three-dimensional paint which is activated by heat. Leave it to dry and then iron on the reverse side between layers of baking paper. This will raise the surface. A heat tool can be used as an alternative to the iron to activate the paint while it is still wet.

Bonding agents (fusible webbing)

Fusible webbing is the collective name for Bondaweb, WunderUnder, Fuse FX, Gossamer Fuse and Misty Fuse. Use these products to bond heat transfer foil to a surface. It is much easier than applying glue.

Heat transfer foil

Always use foils with the colour side up. Cover the foil with baking paper and iron onto a fusible webbing background with a medium iron. After ironing, remove the cellophane carrier sheet before continuing.

Fabrics

Scrim: The scrim used for the samples in this book was a very lightweight, openweave cotton fabric.

Tyvek paper: A very strong spun bonded material which does not tear but can easily be cut with scissors. It is available as fabric and paper in several different weights and thicknesses. Medium-weight Tyvek paper was used for the samples in this book.

It can be stitched very easily and, when heated with a hot air tool or an iron, it shrinks, bubbles and distorts giving a huge variety of wonderful textures. With care it can also be machine stitched after heating.

Although waterproof, Tyvek takes wet and dry colouring medium very well. It can be coloured before or after heating but make sure the colouring medium you use is heat-proof.

Vilene polyester fabrics: These include Craft Vilene, Lutradur and Evolon. They all produce very different and exciting results which are covered fully later in the book.

SECTION 1:
Creative Surfaces with Scrim

As you go through the book, you'll find lots of ways to create textured and background surfaces. One that I find particularly exciting is scrim (cheesecloth) combined with acrylic paints, gesso, foils, Tyvek, Xpandaprint and various other mediums.

Although most of these surfaces will work well on their own, they will all be enhanced if further embellishment is added in the way of stitch, beading or additional mixed media products and techniques.

The scrim used throughout the book is a very lightweight open-weave cotton fabric.

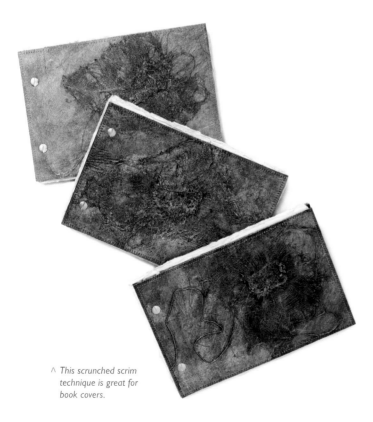

∧ *This scrunched scrim technique is great for book covers.*

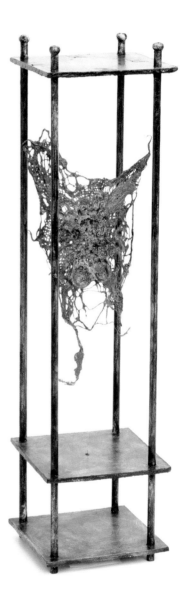

∧ *This three-dimensional piece was made with scrunched scrim and a constructed frame for a free-flowing effect.*

Scrunched scrim

This textured surface was created by bonding scrim to Tyvek, then pressing with a hot iron. This caused the Tyvek to shrink which in turn scrunched the scrim and adhered it to the Tyvek. The finished piece was applied to a firm background such as Craft Vilene or a heavyweight Lutradur before adding a layer of gesso followed by fluid acrylic paints.

Here's how:

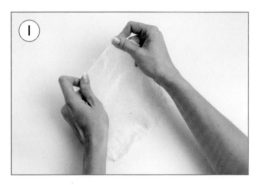

1. Take a piece of scrim about 15 cm (6 in) square and distress the edges by gently pulling out some of the threads. 15 cm (6 in) is about the right size to decorate a postcard and an ideal size to start practising this technique.

2. Lay the scrim on baking paper and iron a piece of fusible webbing (Bondaweb) about 7 cm (about 2¾ in) square in the centre. The Bondaweb is placed in the centre of the scrim so that you can distress the edges further after scrunching, if you wish. As scrim is an openweave fabric, always make sure to lay it on baking paper before bonding as some of the adhesive will go right through the fabric.

3. Cut a piece of Tyvek about 1 cm (just over ¼ in) larger than the fusible webbing and trim around the edges to make an organic shape. You will find that the resulting melted Tyvek will have a more pleasing shape if you cut in this manner rather than cutting it square or with hard edges.

4. Peel the backing sheet from the fusible webbing and lay the Tyvek on top. Flip the whole piece over so the Tyvek is directly on the baking paper with the scrim on the top. Cover with baking paper.

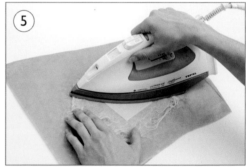

5. With the iron on the cotton setting, slowly stroke it across the surface of the Tyvek. No need to press hard. You may find this technique gives a better result if you stroke the iron across the surface several times rather than holding it down in one place for a few seconds. In order to illustrate this step more clearly, we have used a small piece of white baking paper over the Tyvek.

6. You will be able to see the Tyvek shrinking through the baking paper so stop when you feel it has shrunk enough – don't be tempted to go too far or the Tyvek will disappear altogether in places.

Here is the finished piece. The distorted Tyvek left concave shapes on the surface.

This sample (right) has a slightly looser texture. Instead of flipping the piece over, the Tyvek formed the top layer and was covered with baking paper and ironed. The sample now has convex shapes on the surface. Before colouring, the surface must be covered with gesso. Why not make a postcard to practise the technique?

∧ *The finished piece of scrunched scrim.*

∧ *Detail of finished scrunched scrim showing convex and concave Tyvek bubbles.*

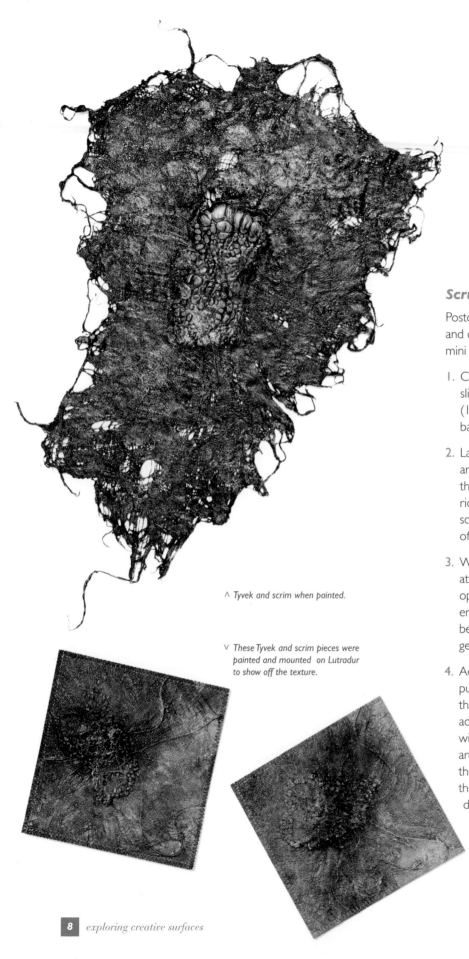

∧ Tyvek and scrim when painted.

∨ These Tyvek and scrim pieces were painted and mounted on Lutradur to show off the texture.

Scrunched scrim postcard

Postcards are great as a reminder of techniques and colourways. They also make really good mini presents. To make:

1. Cut a piece of Lutradur or Craft Vilene slightly larger than postcard size (15 × 10 cm, 6 × 4 in). This will be your backing fabric.

2. Lay the scrunched scrim piece on the surface and arrange the outer edges of scrim so that they lie as flat as possible without any hard ridges. Don't worry about the edges of the scrim overhanging as these will be trimmed off later.

3. Work some stitch on the scrim piece to attach it to the backing fabric. This is an ideal opportunity to use up all those odds and ends of threads as colour isn't important because the surface will be covered with gesso in the next step.

4. Add gesso to the surface. Use a brush to push the gesso into the scrim to make sure that the whole fabric is coated but don't add too much gesso or some of the texture will be lost. Lift the edges of the scrim that are not held down with stitch and push the gesso underneath before adding more through the surface. Be careful that the gesso does not puddle around any high stitches, especially if a thick thread is used. Leave to dry thoroughly.

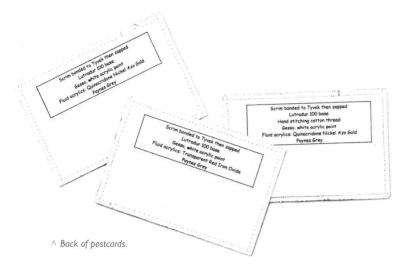

^ Back of postcards.

The stitch can be omitted. In this case just miss out step 3.

The surface can now be coloured with whichever colouring medium you prefer.

> Procion dye in Indigo Navy and Rust Brown was used for this piece.

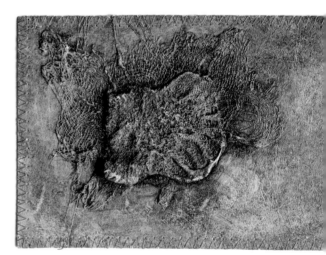

> This piece shows how effective fluid acrylic paints can be.

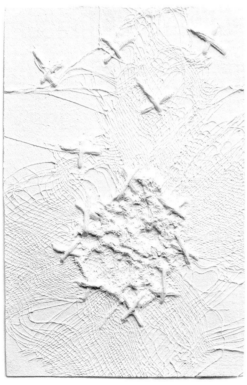

^ Stitch has been added to the scrunched scrim postcard before layering with gesso.

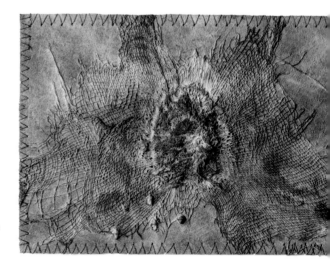

> Black writing ink with bleach dribbled over the surface.

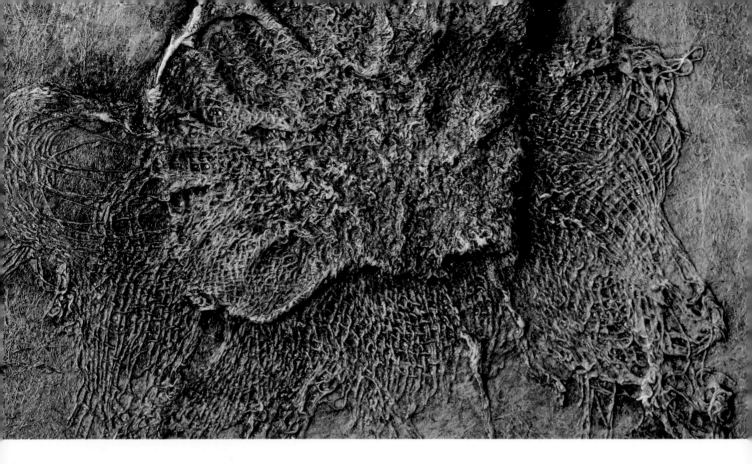

Fluid acrylic paints

These are great for surface colour with this technique, see photo above. You can use them directly on the gesso but it is preferable to add a layer of white acrylic paint to the gesso, allow it to dry thoroughly and then apply fluid acrylics. The layer of white paint allows you more time to work your paints on the surface. Bear in mind the following:

- Acrylic paints from a tube or pot (generally known as heavy body acrylics) can be applied directly to the gesso surface without the layer of white paint.
- Different finishes can be achieved by allowing the first layer of colour to dry thoroughly before adding further colour or working wet into wet.
- A light spray of acrylic varnish can be applied to seal the surface.

There are other ways of colouring the scrim. Try Procion dye, silk paint or ink. When your sample is finished, trim the edges down to postcard size, mount on heavy watercolour paper and machine stitch around the edges with a zigzag stitch.

Then add a label on the back with brief notes of technique, materials and colours used. This is a very good practice as you will then have something to jog your memory if you decide to use the same technique at a later date. It can be very frustrating to find a gorgeous sample a few months later and forget exactly how you achieved it.

If for some reason the samples do not lend themselves to being made into postcards, a swing ticket label with brief details can be attached.

< Finished pieces made from the Tyvek and scrim technique.

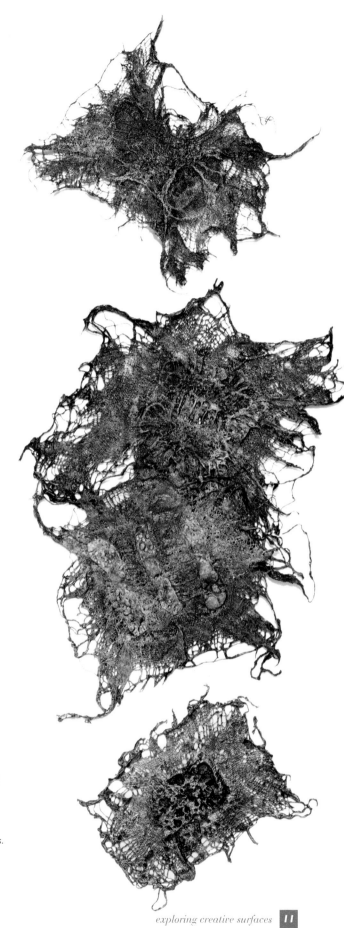

> Scrunched scrim was used to create these samples, suitable for free-hanging pieces. Both sides were coated with gesso and coloured with acrylic paints.

Further ideas for scrunched scrim

Scrunched pieces of scrim in various sizes can also be applied to a quilted surface before colouring.

The boxed frame for the hanging shown was rescued from a used canvas that was no longer required. The original canvas had been removed, ready to be replaced with a new piece of work.

∨ *Scrunched scrim applied to a quilted surface.*

The fabric is duck cotton or heavy calico that was machine stitched to a background, in this case, an old blanket, to give it a slightly padded effect.

The scrunched scrim was applied to this background with additional hand stitch before wrapping around the canvas and stapling in place. The surface was then covered with gesso. White acrylic paint, applied to the surface of the gesso, gave the perfect base for painting with fluid acrylic paints.

The scrunched scrim pieces could be painted before attaching to a background or could be left as free-hanging pieces. To make these, work like this:

1. Lay the piece on a plastic sheet and apply a layer of gesso.

2. Lift and move onto a second sheet of plastic. If you leave to dry in the same place, a skin will form where the gesso had been applied over the edges. If this does happen, you can usually rub it off once the gesso is dry.

3. When dry, flip the piece over and apply gesso to the reverse side. Colour as before.

4. If the finished piece is intended to be seen from both sides, suspend the piece after colouring both sides. This will prevent the underside from drying on the plastic as that can leave the surface shiny in places, especially if using acrylic paints.

> *Detail of a free-hanging scrunched scrim piece.*

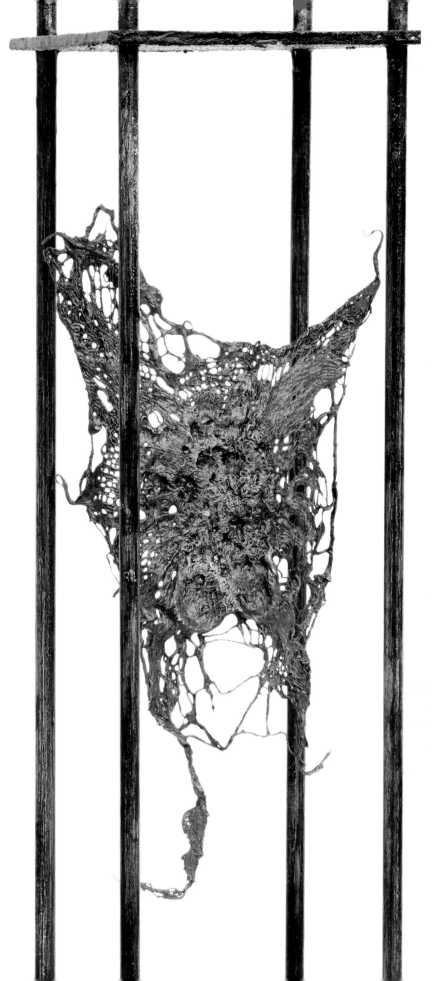

∧ Heat Distress Tissue was bonded to scrim with fusible webbing and ironed on the cotton setting, which caused the tissue to shrink. Gesso was then applied to the surface.

< As this lacy fabric is quite open, the Tyvek was coloured first before bonding to the back. This helped prevent any white patches showing through the lace.

< Polyester velvet scrunched with Tyvek.

Using coloured scrim

This scrunching technique will also work well using pre-coloured scrim.

- The Tyvek will need to be coloured too or patches of white may show through.
- Use whichever medium you prefer to colour the Tyvek to match the scrim.
- These pieces can now be worked into further with stitching or beads or could be added to a larger project.

Scrim with other heat reactive materials

Try the same technique but experiment with Heat Distress Tissue or Lutradur in place of the Tyvek. The scrim will scrunch up differently with these materials but will still give a textured surface that can be finished in the same way.

Try a variety of lightweight fabrics, working like this:

1. Iron fusible webbing to the reverse side of the fabric.

2. Cut the Tyvek in the same way as before and position it underneath the fabric.

3. Place baking paper over the top and iron. You should be able to see the fabric start to scrunch up through the baking paper.

Although it is a slightly thicker material, muslin can be used in the same way as scrim and lends itself well to the application of gesso, acrylic paints and other colouring mediums.

A lightweight Lutradur can be used in place of the Heat Distress Tissue to give a similar effect. However, this would need to be zapped with a heat tool, rather than heated with an iron, to make the Lutradur shrink.

Foiled scrim

Scrim is also exciting when used with heat transfer foil.

1. Lay out a piece of scrim as smoothly as possible (it may be necessary to iron it first) and place it on top of baking paper. Use an iron set at 'wool' (warm setting) to attach Bondaweb to the surface. Remove the backing paper from the Bondaweb.

2. Place the heat transfer foil, coloured side up, on top of the Bondaweb, cover with another sheet of baking paper and run the iron slowly across the surface.

3. Now gently peel the cellophane carrier sheet from the foiled surface – this can sometimes be quite tricky.

Here are some ideas for using it:
- The scrim could be coloured before the transfer foil is applied or it could be painted afterwards with fluid acrylic paints or Procion dyes. If painted with Polymer Medium first, the colours will be brighter.
- Painted scrim could be bonded to coloured Craft Vilene before bonding heat foil to both surfaces.
- Coloured scrim could have transfer foil bonded with FuseFX or Mistyfuse for a lighter effect.
- Foiled scrim can be moulded into shape by painting it with Polymer Medium or PVA glue. Do this on a plastic sheet. It can be manipulated with your fingers or the end of a brush.

> The top two samples show the use of Procion dye over foil. The exciting effects of scrim bonded with an adhesive to coloured and foiled Craft Vilene can be seen in the next sample. Manipulated scrim can be seen at the bottom, before and after painting.

SECTION 2:
Creative Surfaces for Three-dimensional Work

This section examines the use of a simple technique with easily obtainable materials, mostly just tissue paper and acrylic mediums. These are used to make a brilliant textured surface, providing a base fabric which is particularly suitable for three-dimensional pieces.

∧ Torn tissue paper strips, bonded both sides to Lutradur with gesso scraped over the surface, were coloured with black writing ink sprinkled with sea salt. The fabric was used to construct the three-dimensional tower. Seen from above, the tower forms a tunnel through which a message can be glimpsed at the bottom.

Making the base fabric

To make a base fabric which is particularly suitable for constructed textiles, tissue paper is bonded to a background fabric with fusible webbing before adding an acrylic medium. A variety of paint finishes are then applied to make a fabric on which to add hand or machine stitching and other embellishments. When cut into pieces, it can be formed into shapes for a larger project.

Unless stated otherwise, the samples and finished pieces seen here are all worked on Craft Vilene or Lutradur, using old dressmaking pattern tissue paper.

Other fabrics such as muslin and calico can be used, together with a variety of tissue papers. The fabrics and the tissue papers will all take up the colour differently, so you could get different finishes with a range of fabrics and tissue papers, even with exactly the same colours.

> Vessel using dressmaking tissue paper with Molding Paste on the top section and stitched and zapped Kunin felt at the bottom. Both surfaces were coloured with fluid acrylic paints.

You will need to decide which background fabric you are going to use, depending on the finished project you have in mind. Some of the mediums still remain quite flexible, even after colouring, so the background fabric will have some bearing on your finished item. Here are three ways to bond the tissue paper to the background fabric. All give slightly different results:

- Bond the tissue paper to the background fabric in one piece.
- Tear the tissue paper into strips before bonding to the surface.
- Scrunch up and then flatten the tissue before bonding to the background to give extra texture.

Experiment with as many different acrylic mediums as you can. Light or Regular Molding Paste and gesso work really well. You could also use Pumice Gel, Garnet Gel, Granular Gel, Fibre Paste, Glass Bead Gel or any of the gel mediums available.

For a cheaper alternative to a textured acrylic medium, try mixing a small amount of fine sand with gesso. This will give you a fine gritty paste.

Method 1

Working on the sample with the complete sheet of tissue paper bonded to the surface, lightly scrape your chosen medium across the surface leaving some of the tissue paper clear. This will give you a variation in colour at the next stage. Leave a few peaks and troughs across the surface as this will also give you a variation in colour:

- Try pressing a rubber Molding Mat or stamp into the acrylic medium to leave an impression. Remember to wash your equipment as soon as possible after using it with the mediums.
- Or you could use a stencil, mask or Thermofax screen to print a design on the surface. This looks particularly effective after scraping a layer of medium across the surface first.
- Another idea would be to use one type of medium for the background and another for the stencil. A different finish will be achieved on each medium once you add colour.

> *The sample at the top shows tissue on a Lutradur background with gesso applied to the surface. Fluid acrylic paint was used as the colouring medium.*

Then you can see the result of a whole piece of dressmaking pattern tissue paper bonded to Lutradur.

The next two pieces show tissue paper, torn into strips and bonded to the surface. The lower of these has Molding Paste applied. Finally we see the whole dressmaking tissue paper piece with Molding Paste.

Gather
Froncer
Zwischen
⅝"(1·5cm) seam allowed
Rentrees
Mit saumzugabe

fabric

FOLD
PLIURE DU TISS

UR DE PLI
GEN DE COST

Gather
Froncer
Zwischen

seam all
Ren
M sau

Method 2

Using the sample with the torn pieces of tissue paper, add your medium in the gaps between the pieces and just slightly overlap it onto the tissue paper. Any background fabric or fusible webbing not covered by the medium will also help to give you a variation in colour.

Before we move on to the exciting business of adding colour to these samples, consider trying these methods of applying tissue to the background:

- The tissue paper can be scrunched up before being bonded to the surface without flattening it out too much. The acrylic medium is then applied lightly to the surface.
- A 'distressed' effect can be achieved by lightly scraping Molding Paste or gesso onto the tissue paper background then using a piece of textured wallpaper to press into the surface and pull back.
- The piece of wallpaper, which will retain some of the medium on the surface, can then be coloured and used as a textured sample.
- Printed tissue paper can give a very pleasing result. Always use a toner-based print on the tissue paper. If you do not have access to a laser printer or photocopier, you can always use a waterproof marker pen to write or draw on the tissue paper before applying the mediums.

< At the back of these samples, you can see bonded tissue paper with Molding Paste. A rubber stamp mat was pressed into the surface immediately after the medium was applied.

< The coloured samples show (top and bottom) the effect of fluid acrylic paints. The middle piece shows the result of scraping white acrylic paint over the surface, with a spray of coloured Procion dye as a final touch.

Colouring

Fluid acrylic paints can be used directly on the textured surface but will soak through to the background fabric quite quickly, leaving the colours fairly dull in places. Applying a medium such as Acrylic Wax, Polymer Medium or PVA first will help make the colours appear more vibrant.

Another alternative is to lightly brush or scrape a layer of white paint across the surface, just catching the peaks. When the colour is added, this option will give you yet another variation in tone.

Gel Medium can also be used to seal the surface before applying fluid acrylic paints.

Gel Medium dries clear, so any pattern markings on the dressmaking tissue paper will still be seen.

Different colouring media will, of course, give you lots of diverse effects. Try to experiment with as many colouring products and types as you can, in some cases combining one or more mediums until you find an effect that is ideal for the project you are working on.

∧ Postcards made using tissue and Molding Paste are extremely effective. Remember that they can be very useful to jog the memory if the painting method is described on the reverse.

Why not try some of those shown in the above samples?

(1) **Walnut ink** gives a wonderful aged look to the surface. Try sprinkling sea salt into the wet walnut ink. Fluid acrylic paints can then be layered on top of the walnut ink.

(2) **Brusho powders** can be diluted in warm water and used as watercolour paint. Brusho colours are really vibrant. Try sprinkling the powders onto the surface and then spraying with water to see the effects you can achieve. You could also use Koh-i-Noor paints as these are the solid block form of Brusho powder.

(3) **Resists** are always fun: rub Markal Paintstiks or wax crayons over the raised areas of the textured surface before washing with any of the above colouring agents. The wax will act as a resist.

(4) **Procion dye** gives an interesting effect. Mix a heaped teaspoon of dye powder with a pint of warm water for a medium shade and use as watercolour paint. No need to add fixatives but be aware that the dye solution will still stain your hands and clothes.

(5) **Silk paints** can be watered down slightly before use. A torn tissue background can look stunning as the surfaces all take the paint differently. Try spraying the colours on rather than brushing and add a sprinkle of sea salt which will give you further patterning.

(6) **Writing ink** can also be sprinkled with sea salt or you could try spraying household bleach onto the inked surface. You can get a different effect by spraying the bleach into wet ink or waiting until the surface is dry.

(7) **Printed tissue paper** can also be used to great effect. This piece has been printed with a laser printer before medium was applied. If you don't have a laser printer try a lettering stamp with a waterproof ink pad or write on the paper with a waterproof marker pen.

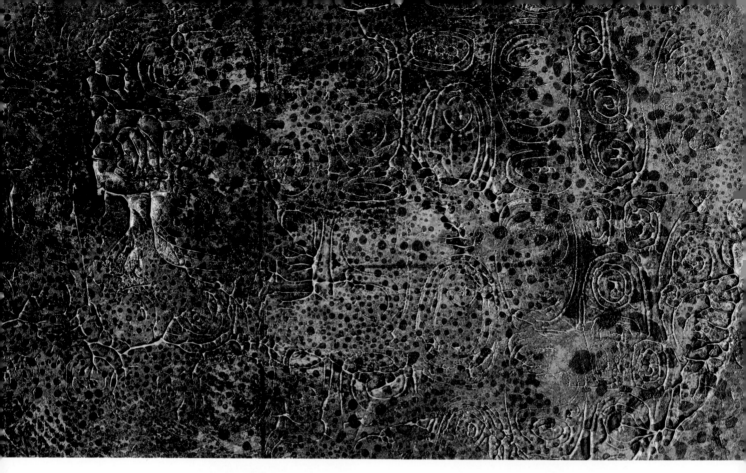

Metallic surfaces

The piece above was made using the white spirit technique to add a metallic look to the textured surface. Work like this:

1. Add a layer of metallic acrylic paint and, when dry, rub generously with Treasure Gold or similar wax. Soak a cotton-wool pad with white spirit and wipe over the surface.

2. Take care not to rub off the Treasure Gold completely; just smear it around the surface. Before the white spirit evaporates, spray very generously with Creative Sprays or similar and leave to dry overnight.

3. When thoroughly dry, spray the surface with acrylic varnish to prevent the spray rubbing off. A brush could be used to apply the varnish although this moves the spray colour around on the surface. However, this too can give a pleasing effect.

4. Try colouring the surface with Procion dye or walnut ink and sea salt before using the white spirit technique.

Two-tone foil effect with Lutradur

This method does not use tissue paper but it does provide a great metallic surface. Although the method used here is similar to the one we used for the scrim, it varies in some ways, so read through the following instructions which will guide you towards the production of some great two-tone effects. These can be achieved using the simple technique of bonding foil to a background and then working with fluid acrylic paints.

Lutradur tends to work best, simply because it is a spun bonded polyester fabric. This means that when you apply foil to the surface, the foil is very patchy and not a solid block as it would be with a closely woven fabric. You are aiming for a patchy look with the foil so that when you apply colour to the surface, it will sink down into the background fabric, as you can see on the opposite page.

Bonding foil to the background fabric

You will need two pieces of Bondaweb and one piece of heat transfer foil cut to the same size as your background fabric, plus a smaller piece of foil in a contrasting colour.

Colouring the background fabric before foiling will give a greater depth of colour to the finished piece. To colour the fabric, use any of the wet media previously mentioned in a mid to dark shade:

1. With the iron on a medium heat setting, bond the fusible webbing to your prepared background fabric.

2. To obtain the cracks and creases in the Lutradur, use the hottest setting when ironing on the first layer of Bondaweb. As the Bondaweb heats, it shrinks slightly and therefore makes the Lutradur crease up. Turn the iron down to a medium setting before applying the foils.

3. Remove the backing paper from the Bondaweb and lay a sheet of foil, shiny side up, onto the surface. Cover with baking paper and press with the iron. There is no need to press hard as it is the heat, not the pressure, which will transfer the foil to the surface.

4. Leave to cool, then remove the cellophane carrier paper from the foil.

5. Now place the second sheet of Bondaweb, sticky side down, on top of the foiled surface and iron once again.

6. You will have to work quite quickly for this next stage as the Bondaweb needs to remain hot for the technique to work correctly.

7. While the Bondaweb is still hot, remove the backing paper, take the second piece of coloured foil and, **with the shiny side up at all times,** just dab it on the surface pressing with your fingertips, just here and there, so that you end up with a two-tone patchy effect.

If the surface has cooled down before you are able to transfer as much of the second colour foil as you would like, just replace the backing paper from the Bondaweb, reheat with the iron and repeat the process.

∧ Two-tone foil effect on a
Lutradur background. The
leaves were made using
the same technique on
Evolon fused to acrylic
felt and cut with a
soldering iron.

When you feel you have transferred enough of the second colour of foil, place a sheet of baking paper over the surface and give it a quick iron to make sure the foil has bonded into the background.

Use fluid acrylic paints to add colour to the foiled surface as they will still enable you to see the warm glow of the foil beneath. Apply the paint in layers, making sure each layer is thoroughly dry before adding the next. Try not to over-brush as this may lift the acrylic paints off the surface.

The other alternative is to brush or spray a sealer over the foiled surface **before** applying the paint. This will make the final piece of fabric slightly stiffer but will still enable you to stitch through it either by hand or machine.

Adding wet media, such as writing ink or walnut ink, to the foiled surface before colouring with fluid acrylic paints will give a different finished effect. Flood the colour on the foiled surface and leave in situ to dry. Once dry, paint with fluid acrylic paints and finish with a light spray of acrylic varnish to seal the surface.

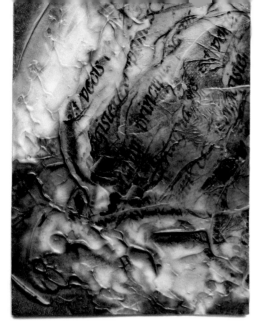

∧ Encaustic wax applied to a Molding Paste surface that has been coloured with Procion dye.

∧ Scrim was laid into a wet medium before colouring to add texture to the flat surface.

Encaustic wax

Back with the tissue surfaces, clear encaustic wax can be melted and brushed over the coloured surface to encase it and help to lift the colour, leaving it with a lovely waxy shine.

Scrim

Layering scrim on the surface before colouring gives an added dimension to a piece of work. Lay the scrim into the wet medium, adding further medium on top. When colouring, be sure to cover all the fibres of the scrim.

> This book has a cover made from applied tissue paper and Molding Paste.

∨ Large pot with scrunched scrim pieces as high relief decoration.

Casts made with dressmaker tissue paper pulp using rubber moulds and Molding Mats.

Paper pulp from dressmaking tissue paper

Once you start using dressmaking tissue paper in your work, you will find you have lots of off-cuts and small pieces left over. Don't throw these away but recycle by making them into pulp. It's very simple to do:

1. Tear the required amount of tissue paper into small strips and place in a bowl or bucket.

2. Pour boiling water over the top and leave to stand for about two hours.

3. To break the tissue paper down to make the pulp, you will need an electric food blender.

4. Take a small handful of the wet paper and place in the blender. Add enough cold water to cover the paper and blend for around thirty seconds. Pour the contents into a strainer and squeeze out as much water as possible. Your pulp is now ready to use.

To make perfectly formed sheets of recycled paper, you will need a mould and deckle which you can buy from paper-making suppliers. However, a good alternative is to spread a thin layer of the pulp on a piece of plastic mesh, the sort used for felt making, and leave it to dry. It will probably take a couple of days. If you wish to write on the paper, you will need to seal the surface first with size.

> A book made from recycled
> dressmaking pattern tissue paper.
> The recycled paper that was
> used for the pages can also be
> seen here.

As with all papermaking you can mix tea-leaves,
dyed moss, dried flowers and petals to the pulp
for added interest.

The pulp can also be used with rubber
moulds or Molding Mats to make casts to
use as embellishments.

Push the pulp into the mould, dab the surface
with a dry sponge to help soak up any excess
water and leave to dry. When dry, the casts can
be painted with the colouring media of your
choice. Remember that gesso can be applied
if you are going to use acrylic paints or any of
the other colouring media that have been used
throughout this book.

SECTION 3:
Creative Surfaces with Screens, Stencils and Masks

Screens and stencils add so much to the use of mediums such as Xpandaprint and gesso. You can see from the pieces shown how well they work on those from the previous section.

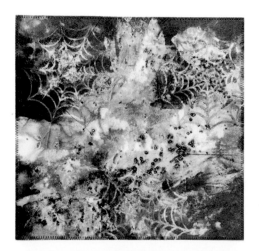

Using a Thermofax screen with Xpandaprint/Puff Paint

A Thermofax screen, stencil or mask used on scrim works well for these techniques. Just make sure you apply any medium as thinly as possible if using a stencil or mask. To use a screen, you will need:

- Blanket, old towel (or something similar) covered with a plastic sheet to make a temporary printing surface.
- Xpandaprint or Puff Paint.
- Small squeegee or old credit/store card.
- Thermofax screen, stencil or mask.

Thermofax screens are available online with pre-printed designs. Some companies will create a screen from your own design, usually at quite a reasonable price, which is useful for computer generated designs. It is great to work from your own inspiration.

When using a Thermofax screen, you will be able to get two or three good prints each time with the same medium before the design starts to smudge at the edges or the medium starts to dry out. When this happens, the screen must then be cleaned immediately. This is very important. Mediums such as Xpandaprint, Gel Medium, gesso etc. will block the holes in the mesh if left to dry, making the screen unfit for use. The screens will last for a very long time if cared for properly. Keep a clean cat litter tray (or something similar) filled with water close by. As soon as it is time to clean the screen, wipe off any excess medium with a baby wipe, then drop it in the water and use a sponge to clean away any residue. Gently pat dry with a kitchen towel and store the screen flat.

∨ *A selection of Thermofax screens, masks and stencils.*

Work like this:

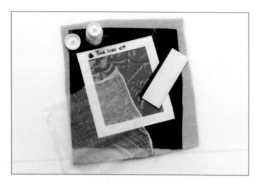

1. Lay a piece of scrim on top of the temporary printing surface. Make sure the scrim is really flat, ironing if necessary.

2. Lay the Thermofax screen on top of the scrim, with the right side facing up. The side of the screen which should be facing up will feel slightly rough compared to the other side.

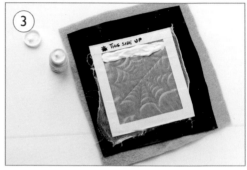

3. Spoon a generous line of Xpandaprint near the top edge of the screen. Be sure to use enough to cover the entire screen in one pull of the squeegee. Any excess can always be scraped back into the pot. With experience, you will be able to gauge how much to use.

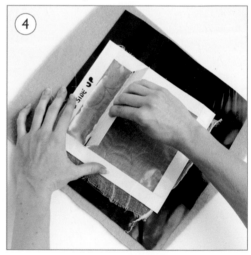

4. Now use the squeegee (or old credit card) to 'push' the Xpandaprint through the screen. Keep the squeegee at a slight angle and use medium pressure. You should only need one pass down the screen as there is a tendency for the Xpandaprint to smudge the edges of the design if the pass is repeated.

Carefully lift the screen from the scrim.

< Scrim was screened with Xpandaprint and painted.

> Xpandaprint design on scrim and Lutradur using a Thermofax screen. The Lutradur was zapped after screen printing.

Remember to wash your screen, stencil or mask immediately after use. However, before you do, try scraping the excess Xpandaprint back into the pot using this method:

- Lay the screen, mask or stencil right side up onto a sheet of kitchen towel (paper towel).
- Use the squeegee to pull down the screen, mask or stencil several times collecting the excess paste and return this to the pot.
- Now gently lift the screen, mask or stencil from the kitchen towel and you will find that you have yet another print.
- This can then be expanded using a heat tool or iron and coloured giving even more surfaces for experimental play.

If Thermofax screens, masks or stencils with an appropriate design are not available then you could try:

- drawing your design on Lutradur and using a brush to apply the Xpandaprint.
- cutting a design from card, Tyvek paper or sticky-back plastic to use as a temporary mask.
- with masking tape, mask off the areas that you wish to be left free of Xpandaprint.

The Xpandaprint can now be activated. There are two ways to do this: with a heat tool or, when dry, by ironing on the reverse side.

∧ Excess Xpandaprint printed onto kitchen towel.

Heat tool method

You can activate the Xpandaprint with a heat tool while it is still wet. Place the scrim on a heat protective sheet/mat. Slowly move the heat tool backwards and forwards over the Xpandaprint area. There is a possibility that the scrim will scorch but, if you are going to cover the surface with gesso and acrylic paints, this will not make any difference.

Iron method

The Xpandaprint needs to be thoroughly dry before ironing. Place baking paper on your ironing surface. Lay the scrim face down and cover with a second piece of baking paper. Use the iron on a wool/cotton setting and gently iron across the surface until the paste has expanded. Do not press hard.

Using a mask or a stencil

The method for using a mask or a stencil is the same as using a Thermofax screen.

Prepare your printing surface, lay the scrim on top and put the stencil or mask in place. Scrape the Xpandaprint through the stencil or mask as sparingly as possible. The results will be slightly different as the Xpandaprint will be more pronounced. Make sure you wash your equipment immediately after use.

Use the colouring medium of your choice to finish the samples. You will find lots of ideas on page 36. Consider bonding the scrim to a background fabric before colouring to give more scope for using the finished pieces.

Double take

If you look back at your printing surface, you will see that because the scrim is an open-weave fabric, the excess Xpandaprint has gone right through the fibres and left an imprint on the plastic.

So why not get two prints for the price of one? This can be done by printing two layers of scrim together and separating them afterwards so that you have a print on each.

∧ *Xpandaprint on kitchen towel bonded to Craft Vilene, then painted with fluid acrylic paints. A layer of gesso was added to the surface before colouring.*

Alternatively, try the following:

1. Lay a piece of Lutradur (the heavier weights are best) underneath the scrim and use the Thermofax screen, stencil or mask with Xpandaprint in the same way as before.

2. Lift away the scrim and you will find a print on the Lutradur. The Xpandaprint design may not be quite as sharp as it might be if you were to screen print directly onto this surface but you will still get a good result.

3. Craft Vilene could be used in place of the Lutradur but bear in mind that if you use the heat tool method to activate the Xpandaprint, there is a possibility the Vilene will buckle with the heat. It can be safely ironed, however, adjusting the iron temperature accordingly.

4. Concentrate the heat on the Xpandaprint areas as much as possible before zapping the background.

For this technique to work successfully on Lutradur, you will need a screen, mask or stencil with an interlocking design. Think of cut-work techniques where pieces remain in contact with each other, see below.

Alternatively, you could machine stitch the Lutradur in a grid pattern, using a cotton thread, before printing your design with Xpandaprint. This will hold it together when it is heated and some areas disappear.

Zapping the Lutradur

The Lutradur will be affected by the heat when the paste is expanded using the heat tool method. Although it is possible to keep the background intact (by leaving the Xpandaprint to dry and then using the iron method), zapping the Lutradur can be exciting. It will lead to some very interesting effects.

< Zapped Lutradur and
Xpandaprint coloured
with fluid acrylic paints.

< Sample coloured with
walnut ink and sprinkled
with sea salt.

Colouring techniques

Acrylics: Add a layer of gesso to the surface before colouring with acrylic paints. Do not apply the gesso or the paints too thickly or some of the texture will be lost. Acrylic paints can be applied directly to the surface but you may find they are rather dull.

Silk paints/Brusho powders/Procion dye/inks: Lay the sample on a plastic surface and use a brush to flood with colour. Leave to dry *in situ* so that the fabrics draw the colour back through to the surface while drying.

Oilbars/Waxes: Try rubbing Markal Paintstiks (Shiva) or wax crayon on the surface before flooding with wet media.

Pieces printed on scrim and kitchen towel can be dipped directly into the dyes or silk paints before leaving to dry.

∧ Markal Paintstik rubbed
on surface before
colouring with Brusho.

Overlays and fragments

Time to consider how some of the pieces could be used to build up into resolved items. Here are some ideas:

- When dry, the zapped and coloured Lutradur pieces lend themselves well to being laid over or bonded to a variety of different surfaces.
- There is also the option of bonding the prepared Lutradur sample to a background **before** colouring.

A foiled background can look particularly effective and will also work with the scrim samples.

> *Gesso onto Lutradur through a Thermofax screen. Zapped and coloured with Procion dye. Gesso design then coloured in with metallic acrylic paint. Mounted on a foiled background.*

> *Gesso onto Lutradur through a Thermofax screen. Zapped and coloured with silk paints.*

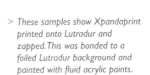

> *These samples show Xpandaprint printed onto Lutradur and zapped. This was bonded to a foiled Lutradur background and painted with fluid acrylic paints.*

< *Lutradur book cover printed with Xpandaprint through a Thermofax screen and zapped with a heat tool.*

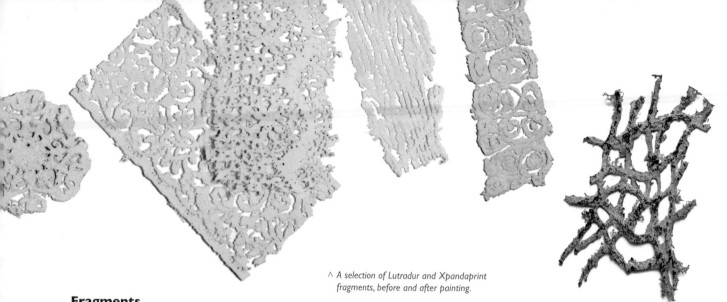

∧ A selection of Lutradur and Xpandaprint
fragments, before and after painting.

Fragments

Zapped pieces, especially those that may have
fallen apart, can be used as fragments and
incorporated into larger projects.

You could always cut fragments from a whole
piece with a soldering iron.

Stitching before zapping

Stitching the Lutradur before zapping will give
more control over the process as the stitching
will act as a resist. Consider the following:

- A cotton thread will remain whole and give
  a more defined background pattern.
- A polyester or rayon thread will melt in
  places with the heat, leaving a more random,
  irregular pattern on the surface.
- Any colour of thread can be used if you
  intend to colour the piece with gesso and
  acrylic paints. Use up all those part reels.
- The Xpandaprint can be applied either
  before or after stitching. If the Xpandaprint
  is applied beforehand, leave it to dry
  thoroughly and machine stitch around the
  design area before zapping.

> The long panels of this shrine are made from Xpandaprint
printed onto Lutradur through a Thermofax screen. They were
then given a layer of gesso and a layer of white acrylic paint
before being coloured with fluid transparent acrylics.

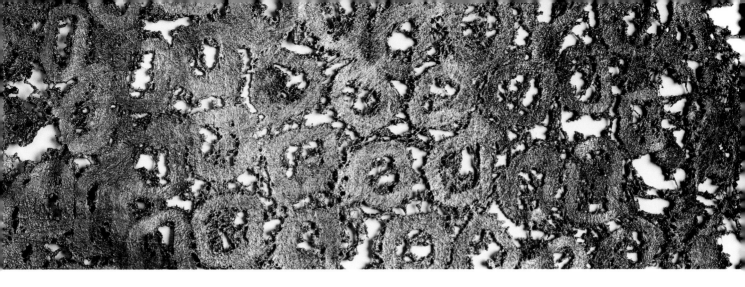

Using gesso or Molding Paste

Gesso or Regular Molding Paste can be used with a Thermofax screen, mask or stencil in the same way as the Xpandaprint in previous samples. Several of the other mediums available can also be used with a mask or stencil but some may be either too thick or too runny to push through a Thermofax screen.

These mediums can also be printed onto various surfaces including the ones used in this book and they work particularly well with Kunin felt that is then zapped.

If printing on Lutradur or Kunin felt you do not have to wait until the medium is dry before you zap. The heat tool will dry the gesso or Molding Paste at the same time as zapping the fabric. However, leaving the mediums to dry then stitching around the outline of the design before zapping will give a more defined pattern area.

∧ *Gesso was used with a Thermofax screen onto Lutradur. It was then zapped and coloured with metallic acrylic paints.*

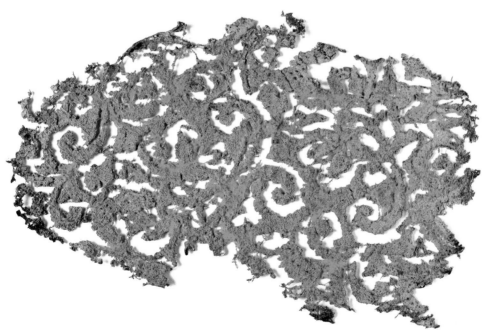

< *This sample shows the effect of zapped Molding Paste with turquoise silk paint and verdigris embossing powder.*

∧ A design was printed
on Lutradur, using a
Thermofax screen. It was
painted with acrylic paint,
foiled and then coloured
with turquoise Procion dye.

Foiling the surface

Carefully iron small pieces of fusible webbing to the areas you wish to foil. Use baking paper to cover your surface as you do not want it to be touched with the hot iron. Lay the foil, colour side up, on the surface, cover with baking paper and iron gently with a warm iron. The piece can be flooded with colour before or after foiling.

You can also apply the foil to a surface which has been coloured with acrylic paints. This will not need any webbing as the binder used in acrylic paints acts like an adhesive and will allow the foil to adhere to the surface.

There are other ways of applying the foil. Try these:

- If only a glimmer of a glittery surface is required, lay the foil on the surface and burnish gently with a metal spoon or something similar.
- Use acrylic paint through your Thermofax screen, stencil or mask. Leave to dry thoroughly then zap the Lutradur back as before. Place the foil over the painted design, cover with baking paper and iron on a medium heat. The foil will not stick to the whole of the painted surface but will cover in a patchy fashion, which is much more interesting. Flood the piece with wet media after foiling for an even better effect.

Surface embellishment

There are many different ways of embellishing the surface of the zapped Lutradur after colouring – a good solution if the colours are not quite what you had hoped for. Try:

- **Embossing powders:** Apply a small quantity of glue to the areas you wish to emboss. Lay the work on a piece of paper, sprinkle generously with embossing powder, shake gently and return the excess to the pot. Heat carefully with a heat tool to melt the embossing powder. Be careful not to overdo it with the heat tool or it may affect the background.
- **Treasure Gold or gilding wax:** Apply sparingly to the raised areas – less is definitely more with this material.
- **Liberon Liming Wax/Verdigris Wax:** Again, apply the wax sparingly to the raised areas. Rubbing on the wax with the fingertips is the best method.

I do hope that you have found lots of ideas in this book that have inspired you and hopefully you will realise the potential for taking these techniques much further and making them your own.